MW00576240

ALL

THAT

YOU

DESERVE

JACQUELINE
WHITNEY

**THOUGHT
CATALOG**
Books

THOUGHTCATALOG.COM
NEW YORK · LOS ANGELES

**THOUGHT
CATALOG
Books**

Copyright © 2021 Jacqueline Whitney.
All rights reserved.

Published by Thought Catalog Books,
an imprint of the digital magazine
Thought Catalog, which is owned and
operated by The Thought & Expression
Company LLC, an independent media
organization based in Brooklyn, New
York and Los Angeles, California.

This book was produced by Chris
Lavergne and Noelle Beams with art
direction and design by KJ Parish.
Special thanks to Bianca Sparacino
for creative editorial direction and
Isidoros Karamitopoulos for circulation
management.

Visit us at thoughtcatalog.com and
shopcatalog.com.

Made in the United States of America.

ISBN 978-1-949759-43-3

*This is your reminder
that you deserve the best of everything,
simply because you exist.*

I want you to know what it feels like to
be in love with the life that you are living.
I want you to know what it feels like to
wake up in the morning and be grateful
for another day, every day. I want you to
have all of the energy you need to live
the life you want to live. I don't want you
to be scared of the unknown—I want
you to see the unknown as a beautiful
puzzle that you will be able to build on
your own. You are capable of building
your dream life—one that you look back
on in the future and are completely in
awe of. I don't want you to look back
and regret not making the move you
doubted you could do. You can do
anything. Start by believing in what you
don't believe you are capable of. Start
by letting go of the strings attached to
your past. Start slowly. It won't happen
all at once but it will happen as it needs
to. Please, don't doubt yourself and
remember you don't need anyone else to
believe in you for your dreams to come
true. You deserve to believe in yourself
and let that energy carry you through.

I hope you choose to
live and not just exist

don't just exist

Please, if there's one thing you do today,
let it be to hold your soul in compassion.
You have been through far too much
to be anything but kind to yourself.

...

Thank you for being the light that shows
others they are not alone. The world truly
would not be the same without you.

...

Please, don't be discouraged.
Trust beyond what you can see.
You are growing and that is good.

...

You are so brave
even if progress feels slow.

...

I hope you choose to fight for yourself instead of
against yourself. I hope you choose to not hold
onto the hurt, but to instead work on the hurt
so that you can live the life you dream about.
I am not saying forgive and forget. Pain often
leaves permanent wounds, but those wounds
will never turn into scars if you never forgive,
and the thing about scars is...scars don't hurt.
Too many people walk around ignoring their
wounds and live a life in a constant fight with
themselves. Life is not supposed to be a repetitive
struggle. Life is supposed to be an enjoyable and
beautiful experience that fills your soul with
more sunshine than rain. You deserve to fight
for yourself and you deserve people who will
fight for you. You are worth someone's complete
attention and care, but this is your reminder
that you are also worth your own. Give yourself
all the time and attention you need to heal.
You are doing better than you think you are.

...

You didn't ask to go through
what you do and you are so
brave for enduring it.

...

You are brave for walking your body out of bed
and for trying to do your best every single day.
You are doing your best. Others don't need to
understand what your best is. You are brave for
trying to move on. You are brave for forgiving that
person that seemed impossible to forgive. You are
brave for giving up on that thing that you never
dreamed you would have to give up on. You are
brave for loving after love broke you. You are brave
for continuing to keep going. Keep going. You are
brave for opening up and speaking about what
felt impossible to speak about. You are brave for
reaching out for help. You are brave for driving
yourself to the appointments you didn't have the
energy to drive yourself to. You are brave for trying
new things that terrify you and don't make sense.
You are brave for moving through the unknown.
You are brave for fighting for yourself and what you
believe is true. You are a brave soul that deserves
to live peacefully in this world. You are brave.

...

You know you are going to get
through this. You always get
through what you go through.

...

You are so brave for loving after love hurt you.

...

You have it in you to become
a version of yourself that you
genuinely love. You have it in you to
become someone you're so proud of.

...

Slowly, you will find your way back to
yourself. You will find yourself alone
one day and finally understand why
everything had to happen how it did.
You will understand that you wouldn't
be the person you are today without the
pains of your yesterdays. I am not saying
everything that happened to you was right
or valid or should have happened. I am
saying you are always strong enough to
become a stronger person because of it.

Those of us who touch darkness and
persevere through it are the ones who
experience more light and goodness
in this life. Some of us choose to not
let what happens to us victimize us,
but instead, change our corners of the
world in any positive way we can. *We
are the changemakers they talk about.*

You don't have to be perfect to be worthy
of being wanted. Be genuine. Be you.

...

Your healing and feelings are valid. You
are allowed to struggle. You are allowed to
feel whatever you are feeling. Sit with your
feelings. Work through them. You must feel
in order to heal. There is no part of you
that is crazy. You are not a burden because
of what you are going through and how
it affects your actions. Someone wants to
support you in all of your emotions. Your
pain does not define you. You will succeed.
You are doing so much better than before.

...

don't hold yourself back
from what you know
is right

You will never feel as loved as you are. You will never understand how loved you are. But that is okay. When you're looking for love in places that lead to a deep-seated feeling of loneliness-go within. Get quiet with yourself. Ask your heart what it needs. It is normal to know there's so much love around you but you still don't feel it. It is normal to always feel like you are lacking something. It is normal to feel like you're missing out on something special. It is normal to not know where to look for love. It is normal to not feel loved. You must consistently connect with yourself first. It must be a daily connection and acknowledgement that everything you feel you are lacking is within you. Everything you ache for can be created within you.

Once your soul has held unexplainable darkness, the world makes it difficult to believe you belong in it. There's nothing more lonely than being around everybody but feeling like nobody can relate to what you experience internally.

So you hold it all in until your soul can't hold it any longer. Maybe feelings you don't want to feel surround you and being awake is exhausting. Maybe no one knows what you are feeling because you don't have the energy to explain yourself. Maybe you don't even know how to put words to what you're going through, and that is so frustrating. Maybe you tell yourself you're overreacting. You're not overreacting—you're going through something difficult.

If you feel like you can't hold it any longer—be gentle with the way you speak to yourself and reach out to someone. Those thoughts that you feel are controlling you—tell them to someone. Someone wants to listen to you. You deserve to be heard. You are not any less than someone you think has it more together than you. You belong here. You deserve to live with a peaceful mind. Be gentle with the way you speak to yourself. You belong here.

Pain always fades.

Please don't be embarrassed about what you've been through. It's difficult to feel like no one truly understands you. It's difficult to feel alone in what you've been through. I promise you, someone in the universe has been through something very similar to you. You are never out of your mind for feeling what you feel. You are never too far gone to be saved.

the way you want to be
treated by someone
is how you have to treat
yourself

As long as you are here, it is not
too late to do the things you wish
you had done by now. Living within
a negative headspace of regret
won't get you anywhere. You will
get to do what you want to do if
you start trying to believe it can
happen. The more negative energy
you put out there, the less positive
outcomes you will get. This is your
reminder to believe in yourself.

You are not too far behind. You are always
growing and going to where you are meant to.

...

You are more capable than you know
and you won't always feel alone.

...

Even if you don't feel like you matter
to everyone, you matter to someone
and that is important to remember.

...

you deserve to feel
the same love that you give

If you need to rest, rest without guilt. There's so much going on in the world all of the time. Sometimes everything feels too heavy. Your body will fight rest because you remember all of the people you feel are being more productive than you. But sometimes the most productive thing you can do is rest. Learning to take care of yourself will only make you more productive in the future.

You deserve someone who will hold your heart through your hard days—someone who won't judge you through it. Someone who will understand that it's okay to not be yourself all of the time. Someone who will still care about you even if time goes by and you haven't reached out to them. You deserve someone who will still reach out to you even when you've been distant. They will know you're going through a hard time, but they will still be there whenever you are ready. You deserve to be transparent without being pushed away. If you haven't found the people you need yet, hold on, because you will. If you have found the people you can't live without, hold onto them and remind them you love them.

it's okay
to not know
right now

Money matters, but not the most.
Pleasure matters, but not the most.
Connection matters. Truth matters.
Memories matter.
Laughter matters.
You matter.

you can do everything
you doubt you can do

and if you try
and you can't
that is okay too

What is it that is holding you back?
Why don't you believe that you are worthy of
what you want? How do you know that waiting
to see if it will even happen isn't worth it?

You deserve to believe in your desires.
You deserve to give yourself a chance.
You deserve to be patient with yourself.

Even if you don't feel it, peace surrounds you. Even if you don't see it, you are doing better than you give yourself credit for. Even if you have no idea what's going on or where you're supposed to be, you are doing better than you think you are. You are not failing if you are trying your best. You are not failing if the results you want aren't showing right now. Even if decisions you make now affect you later negatively, in the end it will be okay anyway.

Choose your truth over fear. Choose to step out on your own knowing that whenever you need support, someone will be there. Choose to choose yourself over anyone else. What is best for you will find you. What is meant to be will come to be. Life is a rhythm of highs and lows and in-betweens, but it is all a part of your story. It all matters.

Because even if something isn't meant to happen, redemption and healing can always happen. Mistakes can always be forgiven. Freedom can always be found. You are free to be whoever you dream to be. You are deeply loved through it all. At the end of the day what matters most is how we make other people feel, how we impact them, how we make their life a little bit brighter every moment we have with them.

Change is scary but change is
necessary. You won't feel ready to
take the next step—the step your
heart has been calling you to, the
one that feels right, even if it's just
a subtle feeling. Something within
you will tell you that you are in
need of change, that you are ready
for new experiences and growth.
You are ready for change when
you constantly feel uncontent
and irritable. You are ready for
change when parts of your past
no longer hold the same pain they
did before. *You are ready for change
even when you don't feel ready.*

you must believe in yourself
just as much and more than
you believe in everyone else

begin to believe and you
will see your life change
in ways you never knew
was possible

I hope you don't give up on yourself because of what someone else did to you.

I hope you don't believe what they did to you was your fault. Maybe you made choices that make you think it was your fault, but you have to remember we don't always make the best decisions when we're doing our best to simply survive. Sometimes when we're living in survival mode we hold onto anyone who holds out a hand even if that hand is deceiving. These are the kind of hands that lie. The kind of hands that touch people for their own pleasure. The kind of hands that get what they want however they want to. The kind of hands that are weak and don't deserve the souls they take advantage of.

The souls they take advantage of are the kind who love more than the love they receive. The kind who don't stop caring about others even if others haven't cared enough about them like they are worthy of. The kind that have been through too much. The kind that are doing their best to keep going even though life keeps beating them down. The kind that everyone wants to know and love. Maybe in the season it happened you were trying to be someone you aren't because being yourself

was too hard. Maybe you were trying to escape
your reality because your reality became too hard
to live in. Maybe what you believe in was used
against you and now you don't know what you
believe in. I hope that no matter what happened
to you, you find the peace to believe in yourself.
I hope that no matter what happened to you, you
know that you can find whole healing. I hope you
offer yourself all the time you need to find your
healing. People will try to make you talk through
it. People will think they know what's best for you
but at the end of the day you are the only one who
knows what's best for you. Trust your instincts.
Trust the inner voice that is nurturing and kind.
More than anything, I just hope you don't give up
on yourself. I hope you don't give up on the dreams
you know you are capable of. I hope you don't
give up on the future you are excited to live with
someone who is incredibly good to you. I hope
you know you will find someone who is incredibly
good to you if you haven't yet. I hope you know
it's not too late to find that someone. It's never too
late to start over because sometimes starting over
is the best decision we'll ever make for ourselves.
You deserve to be held by hands that are pure and
kind. I hope you're proud of the person you are
because you are someone no one could ever be.

I don't think you really know how
loved and valuable you really are.

*This is your reminder that you are
so loved and so valuable.*

you do not have to
please everyone

not everyone deserves
what you have to give

you'll never be enough

for someone

if you aren't enough

for yourself

If today was difficult for you, I hope you know that tomorrow can be better. I hope you know that the moments that are uncomfortable or hurt or don't make sense will pass. I hope you remind yourself of all the times you didn't think you were going to feel better but you did. As you go through your days remember that every moment is just a moment. When you can't take it one day at a time, try to just take it one breath at a time. Take really good care of yourself and know that it's okay if you don't accomplish everything you told yourself you needed to today. You don't have to start a new routine or healthy habit today if it feels like too much. You don't have to be as productive as the people that you see online. Your life is your life and you only have this life. Tomorrow it will feel a little bit better. You are safe. You are being guided. You will have everything that you need.

Creating boundaries between you and someone
bringing negative energy into your life is
never selfish. No matter how close you are to
someone, trust yourself when you know you
need to say *no* or distance yourself. *Please, don't
let anyone get in the way of the peace you deserve.*

...

Hurting someone because they hurt you
will never make you hurt less.

...

Quit if you know you need to quit.
When we leave something we know
isn't meant for us, doors actually
do open. *You can begin again.*

...

not all positive change

feels positive

in the beginning

it is okay
to take as many
moments as you
need for yourself

Whatever doesn't make sense now
will make sense someday.
Whatever hurts now
won't hurt the same someday.
But even if it doesn't, you will still always be okay.

No matter how hard it gets, no matter how hopeless it feels, no matter how much pain fills your being—you will always end up okay. Remind yourself of how far you have come. Remind yourself of the light you found in the darkness. Remind yourself of the strength you found all on your own.

Being okay doesn't always happen right away and maybe it isn't supposed to. Along the way to being okay you will learn to love yourself in a way you never have. You will learn to appreciate so much about who you are—the perseverance your heart holds, the compassion you nurture the world around you with, the gratitude you are made of, the joy you deserve—you will learn what it means to *actually* live.

Sometimes along the way to being okay the best thing you can do is remind yourself that you will always end up okay—even if you don't believe it. Write it down. Make a song with only those six words. Paint the words in a picture or draw them on your skin. Tell someone else they will always end up okay because sometimes reminding others helps us remind ourselves.

tomorrow it will feel

a little bit better

Yes, your feelings are valid—*all of them.*

...

You don't have to understand why you feel
what you feel, but you must talk freely if you
want to break free. You must not hold your
truth back if you want to move forward.
You must say something. Your voice matters
more than you know. No, you are not too
much. No, you are not burdening anyone
with your honesty. No, breaking down is not
weak. Breaking down is possibly one of the
strongest things you can do. Because *breaking
down leads to breakthrough and breakthrough
is how you get through.* You are trying and
that is admirable. If you feel like you are
the only one who sees that you are trying,
that's not true, someone else sees it too.

...

You don't need to regret something you did or someone you were with because in the moment, something within you chose it.

...

Just because their situation may seem worse than yours doesn't mean what you're going through isn't valid. Just because they need support doesn't mean you don't need support, too. Some people might be living through absolute tragedy, but please know, anything at all that you feel doesn't make you selfish. Please, don't be too hard on yourself and your emotions. Feel them. Nurture them. Your struggles are not any less valid than anyone else's. We're all going through something, all of the time.

...

Please, put your mental health before anything or anyone else. Please, do not tell yourself that anything or anyone is more important than your mental health. Please, be extra kind to your mind all of the time. Please, do not stop moving towards freedom. You will find freedom. You are finding freedom. It is not about escaping your mind. It is not about feeling better right away. It is not about proving to other people that you are trying your best to feel better. You are trying your best to feel better and your recognition is the only recognition that matters. You do not have anything to prove to anyone. You do not need to rush your process of finding freedom. The thoughts that are holding your heart tight are just thoughts. They feel so powerful but they are not. They feel so in control but they are not. Your soul is in control. You should always be the first person you run to—check in with yourself. When you need extra help, run to someone else. There should be no guilt attached to needing help. Nothing is more important than you being okay.

Please, be kind to your precious mind.

...

Please, don't give up now. You'll
see why you're meant to be alive.

...

It will get better even if it doesn't feel like it will.

...

even after losing it all
you never lost your resilience
and your resilience is
a really beautiful thing that
can never be taken away from you

Sending love to anyone struggling with
their mental health. I am so proud of you
for doing your best to be okay.

...

There will come a time when the memories
that trigger you now won't trigger you any
longer. You will be alone and fully understand
that you had it in you all along to keep
going. You had the strength in you all along
to fight basically all on your own. You will
remember the faces of the people who helped
you get through, but you will know it was
really you that got you through. You may
not understand why you went through what
you did but you will be a force of healing
in the lives of people you don't realize need
you. Continue fighting for you. You'll see
the light soon. This earth adores you.

...

Your mind is a precious piece of you
that must be taken care of with more
kindness than you give it. Please, do
not listen to the lies it tells you. Do
not listen to the thoughts that tell
you that you are not good enough.
Do not listen to the thoughts that
think you have anyone to compare
yourself to. Do not listen to the
thoughts that think you are not
worthy of tomorrow. Please, remind
your mind that it is precious.
Remind your mind that it works
so hard all of the time and you are
thankful for it. Please, do not judge
your thoughts. Be a friend to them.
Tell the thoughts that are not good
to walk away. Remind your mind
that thoughts are only thoughts.
Your future is filled with so much
goodness. Be kind. Be kind. Be kind.

you are always more loved
than you feel

you have been through so much
but you are still here

you are supposed to be here

It's so normal to see other people
living their lives and feel bad about
yourself because you don't have the
energy to live yours like them. It's so
normal to want to isolate yourself
from the world when you feel like
the world is too much. But please,
don't hide your heart because you
feel like you're too much. You are
never too much for the right people.
If someone makes you feel like
you are too much, maybe they're
not someone you need around.
We so easily convince ourselves
we're a burden even when we're
reminded we're not. People want
to be there for you. People want
to love you. Let them love you.

Find joy in all that you do.

...

It will be alright. Maybe not now, but soon.

...

We never know what someone is going through.
Be really kind to yourself and others, always.

...

You are doing your best and your best is absolutely
enough—no matter what your best looks like.

...

Take a deep breath and let go of whatever
thoughts are making you anxious right now.
You don't need to figure it out right now.

...

As impossible as this might sound, it's very possible you will be thankful for your struggles someday because maybe you'll see it made you into the person you are today.

Maybe everything doesn't happen for a reason or maybe it does, but anything can be turned into something. You get to choose if that something is positive or negative.

you will find yourself through
what you are going through

You do have the strength to change.

...

Choose yourself this time.

...

Every single detail of your life will
work out how it is meant to.

...

You can pull the dreams out of the
box you've held them in and let
them soar. You can be whatever you
dream of being. You can breathe
and be held by the comfort of your
breathing. You can do nothing if
everything feels like too much.
You can let go of the one you're
trying so hard to hold on to. You
can live without them. You can give
yourself all the time you need in your
letting go. You can open your heart
for someone else eventually. You
can love someone and still not want
them in your life. You can outgrow
someone and still love them.

You can stand up for yourself. You
can look up to the sky and know
you are not alone in this world. You
can still do the things you haven't
done. It is not too late. You can be
resilient but still deserve all the
time you need to rest. You can do
anything that you think you can't.

You can.

Keep trusting the journey you are on.

...

What makes you feel really good? What
makes your heart feel filled with love?
What inspires you to live your best
day everyday? What do you need?
You cannot be the best version of yourself
when you are living to please others. You
cannot be the best version of yourself when
you are constantly seeking others' approval.
Choose to step out of your comfort zone
and try something new. Choose to trust
you will be safe. You can always go back
to where you were if it doesn't feel right.
You can always start over. But at least
you can show yourself that you tried.

...

It might not make sense right now. It might feel utterly chaotic and overwhelming. You might feel like sometimes you're living a life that isn't even yours. You might be slowly falling or slowly rising. You might be okay some days and not okay other days. You might not know which way to go—you might think you do then end up realizing it wasn't the right way after all and that is okay.

You're supposed to mess up. You're supposed to get lost and find your way out. You're supposed to find failure in order to find success. What might not make sense right now will make sense when it's supposed to. Please, try to enjoy the journey you're on. Every day wants to show us small glimpses of where we're headed.

The journey isn't always about the career we're going to have or the person we're going to end up with. It's not always about how much money we can make or how many people we can please. Most of the time the journey is an inner experience. Every day we learn something new about ourselves. Every day we are growing. Every day we are becoming who we are meant to be and that is the most important journey of all. You are doing just fine. You are enough through it all. Keep trusting.

do whatever you have to do
to be okay
and trust that it's true
what they say
it's okay to not be okay

One little step at a time.

You are finding your way.

...

You need to keep pushing through.

...

What seems like an insignificant chapter of your life now
may turn into one of the most important ones in the
end. You are rising and blooming into a beautiful story.

...

Please, don't put pressure on yourself to have healed already. We aren't designed to handle too much too soon. Healing can take so many more years than we think it will and that is okay. We aren't designed to handle too much too soon. Our brains don't experience time—we may be triggered by something and instantly feel like we are back in the moment of the traumatic experience. No one has been through what you have. We can relate to other people's stories of struggle because pain is ingrained in the human condition. Healing happens when we relate and feel less alone. There is no map for the mess and wonder healing is. The process will mostly never make sense, but you will figure it out as time goes by. There is no wrong or right amount of time when it comes to healing. There is no wrong or right way to heal.

You deserve to have someone you can be
honest with about your struggles.

...

I hope you find time to remind yourself
that you are where you need to be and you
will get to where you want to be.

...

Don't let another person hold you back
from doing what you know is right.

...

Please, don't live your life by society's expectations. Don't let yourself down because the world makes you feel behind. Where you are in life is good enough. No matter your age, you are here today, so there is time. There is time to quit the job you hate and find one you enjoy. There is time to go back to college if that's what you want to do. There is time to fall in love with the right person. There is time to have a family of your own no matter what that looks like. There is time to learn how to stop losing yourself trying to please others. There is time for growth and for change. There is time for healing and for understanding. As long as you are breathing there is time. Don't rush time. Let it flow how it needs to. Whatever you are rushing or feel like the people around you may be rushing—slow it all down. Don't compare your life to the life of any other. Your life is yours to create.

You can move on from what is
holding your heart back.

...

You can move on, and you will. Take your time
with your moving on. Let it feel messy and
uncomfortable. Let it teach you about love and
about life. The most impactful lessons are learned
through the most difficult experiences. Breakups
are hard. Life is hard. Love is hard. But even
though these things are true, I hope you know
that no relationship is a waste of time. It's not a
waste of time if you break through the breaking,
if you continue moving forward even when the
cracks in your heart are hurting. Heartbreak
leads to a remake of you. You are learning to
love in ways you couldn't love before. Even if
you know they weren't for you, that doesn't
mean it can't hurt. All of your feelings are always
valid. You are strong enough for the breaking.
Who is meant for you will find you. In the
meantime—find yourself. Hold your heart tight
and embrace the growth that the mess makes.
You are growing for the love you are meant to love.

...

Just because you are breaking
does not mean you are not whole.

...

You are someone's favorite person. *Stay for them.*

...

You are a good person even if some
people make you feel like you are not.
Someone's inability to see your worth
does not mean you have no worth.

...

all of your hard work
will lead to a reward
you will make it
you are making it

You don't always have to explain
yourself. It is not your job to make
people understand your heart.

...

I promise, you have a purpose for your life
that hasn't been revealed to you yet. You can
and you must continue trying to find your
path. Someday you will understand why going
to what seems like a dead-end always leads
to an opportunity for something better. *You
are always being guided to what is best for you
if you simply stay open to the possibility that
you will end up where you belong when the time
is right.* For now, I hope you know that you
are growing into who you are meant to.

...

There is someone who will cherish you
for the precious person you are.

...

It is okay to need a break from any kind
of relationship in your life. Sometimes
souls need to breathe on their own for a
little while so that when they catch their
breath again, and *hopefully* take time to
sort themselves out on their own, they can
love more deeply when the time to connect
again comes—if it is meant to. You will
know if you are meant to connect again.

...

it's okay if you can't
handle everything today

Your bad experiences help you understand
what others struggle with and that is powerful.

...

Life is supposed to be wildly exciting. Life is
supposed to be filled with daily unknowns
so that you grow through figuring things
out. Self-love is a continuous, never-ending
journey of choosing yourself over and
over and over again. Self-love is choosing
to choose yourself over anyone else. Why
is it that you so easily love and take care
of others but you don't give yourself even
close to the amount of attention you give
others? This is one of the best qualities
about you. I just hope you realize one day
that you were always worthy of the same
depth of love and more that you give away.

...

I hope you find time to remind yourself
that you are where you need to be and you
will get to where you want to be.

...

I know it's natural to compare your life
to others when social media is a part of
your daily routine. I know being alone can
overflow you with anxiety and overthinking.
I hope you know you have the power to
change the way you think and you have the
strength to accomplish all that you need to.
When you change the way you think and
speak to yourself, you change. Your feelings
change. Your doubts soften and you attract
positive energy. The more positivity you
surround yourself with, the more you will see
your life change for the better. Choose who
you choose to be around with this in mind.

...

what feels never-ending
will end
this is temporary
what feels hopeless
can become hopeful
hold on to your faith
what seems impossible
is possible
believe

I don't know you but I am proud
of you for being where you are.
You have come so far. Life
probably wasn't always easy to
live but you are here despite it all.
You are here and you belong.

I hope you stand in the power your
soul holds. I hope you know there
is a light within you always guiding
you to where you belong. I hope you
know that you are a guiding light for
others and you are so appreciated.

The truth is, life is really delicate and really unpredictable. One day you can be telling someone you love them and the next they are gone. One day you can be in perfect health and the next you are fighting for your life. Most of the time, we walk through our days unconsciously—rushing time as if we have all the time in the world. Most of the time, we are looking towards the future as if the future will be everything we want now, as if this moment right now is never enough, as if we won't be complete until we accomplish what we think will fulfill us. The truth is, we don't know how much time we have left. We don't know if our next breath will lead to death. We don't know if the moments we tell ourselves will happen, will happen. I don't mean to say this to scare you or to be dark. I say this to lovingly remind you that your life is yours to live now. Don't wait. Don't spend your days dreaming without taking action. You are worthy of your dreams but your dreams won't happen without action. Life is fragile but insanely beautiful if you just try to look for the beauty within it no matter what you are going through. No matter how dark it gets, light is always present. Even if you feel fragile, you are insanely strong. Don't forget to live your life the way you want to. Life is meant to be lived, not ignored.

I promise you
you will look back on these days
and be so grateful you made it through
and you will see how much stronger
you are because of these days
and you will wake up feeling grateful
for another day everyday
and you will become someone you are so proud of
let the light break through any darkness
trying to hold onto you
light always comes after darkness

yes
life really is
too short
live now

It's time to start really experiencing life now and it's especially time to stop taking any time you have here for granted. Stop running away from the dreams you've tucked away somewhere far away. Start believing you are worthy of your wildest dreams and you will see your dreams begin to show up in your reality. Stop ignoring the signs showing you what you need to do. Follow the signs with passion. Passion is the path to purpose. Start celebrating the people you care about as if you may never see them again. Time is infinite but the time we have here on this planet is limited. *Live now, not later.*

You won't become someone you
love when you're constantly running
away from yourself. You will never
love where you are now or who you
are now when you are constantly
trying to predict the future. Focus
on what you have now. Focus on
the small changes you can make
now. Preparing for the future is
a good thing to do, but you will
never be happy if you only live
now focusing on the future. You
are where you are and that is
where you need to be right now.

this is your reminder
to stop overthinking
the only place
overthinking will lead you
is nowhere

Ask yourself this:

Who do I feel most like myself around? Who makes me feel more energized than drained? Who doesn't judge me when I'm feeling off? Who encourages me to be the best version of myself I can be without making me feel guilty? Lean into these people. Let go of the ones who bring you down more than they bring you up. Life is too short to put up with people whose energy doesn't align with yours.

Pain can lead to vulnerability. Please don't hold
onto unsafe people in your healing seasons
because you think they will help you escape
from your pain. Safe people are honest. Safe
people don't distance you from the people who
care about you. You have to trust the instincts
within you telling you right from wrong. You
have to listen to the ones who know you the
best. You have to remember that someone who
wants the best for you won't take advantage
of you in any way. Unsafe people will say
anything to make you believe something they
want you to believe so that they can find
pleasure. They sugarcoat any detail they want
to even if it is far from the truth so that they
feel good. Please, if you let someone in who
took advantage of you, don't beat yourself
up. You were doing the best you could to
get through. You were hurting and holding
onto any hope you could. Forgive yourself.
If you are currently in a situation where you
think someone might be taking advantage of
you, don't ignore the red flags. Open up to
someone safe and don't feel embarrassed. You
are strong enough to get through, no matter
how deep into it you are. You deserve better.

One breath at a time. If you can't handle
today, there is always tomorrow.

...

Trying to control what is impossible to
control will never get you to where you want
to be. *Let go of what you cannot control.*

...

Don't stop being kind to other people
because some people hurt you. Be kind to
yourself by slowly forgiving the past and
do something kind for someone today.

...

Whatever it is that you've been holding
in, you don't have to hold it in any longer.
Talk to someone. You will feel better.

...

you can handle more than
you give yourself credit for

It is not about feeling better right away. It is not about proving to other people that you are trying your best to feel better. You are trying your best to feel better and your recognition is the only recognition that matters. You do not have anything to prove to anyone. You do not need to rush your process of finding freedom. The thoughts that are holding your heart tight are just thoughts. They feel so powerful but they are not. They feel so in control but they are not. Once your soul has held unexplainable darkness, the world makes it difficult to believe you belong in it. There is nothing more lonely than being around everybody but feeling like nobody can relate to what you experience internally. You are not alone in that feeling. So you hold it all in until your soul can't hold it any longer. Please, if you feel like you can't hold it any longer—be gentle with the way you speak to yourself and reach out to someone. Those thoughts that you feel are controlling you—tell them to someone. Someone wants to hear you. You deserve to be heard. You are not any less than someone you think has it more together than you. You deserve to feel free.

Sending love to anyone feeling like
they are slipping into depression.
You are safe. You will find your way
through. Be nurturing to yourself.

don't hold yourself back from
what you know is right

this is your sign to let go and go

Never forget life is precious. Please
don't take your breath for granted.
Life is long yet life is short. Tell
them you love them. Make memories
that fill your soul with joy. Take
that leap of faith. Keep going. Hold
each other tight. Fight for yourself
and know that your peace is more
important than anything else.

You matter so much more than anyone could ever make you understand. Relying on others to show you what you're worth will never make you feel fulfilled. Even if you don't believe it, remind yourself that you matter daily.

The thing is,
you are already whole.

...

Although it might be difficult right now, you
have made it through difficult times before.
You will make it through this, too.

...

You should never feel guilty for feeling deeply. You should never feel like you have to hold in your honesty because you are afraid the person you are with will judge you. The way you experience feelings has given you an empathetic heart and your empathy is your power.

The way you experience living changes the moment trauma touches your soul. The way you see other people, the way you navigate relationships, the way you think and process every detail of every experience changes from that moment forward. You may not see the way it changed you right away, you may not like the way it changes you, or you may find yourself overwhelmingly grateful for aspects of your struggles because without the pain you wouldn't have found the purpose you have. Some people become victims of their past that pollute the world with unhealthy negativity. Other people become positive forces of angelic light that touch more souls than they even know. Healing is a choice. Numbing yourself because it seems more comfortable than dealing with the trauma is a choice. The ones who choose healing are the ones who experience heaven on earth. The ones who choose healing are the light workers the world wouldn't survive without. The healing is unfathomably difficult, but the other side is beyond worth it. Which kind of person have you become or do you want to become?

It's not too late to become the person
you've always wanted to become.

...

It is okay to not be healed from something you
thought you healed from.

...

It's okay if today is not your day,
the sun will shine again tomorrow.
It's okay if you don't feel like
yourself today, tomorrow may
bring you back home to yourself.
Feeling lost within yourself isn't
as negative as it feels—feeling lost
may be the very reason you find
yourself, it may be the very reason
you become someone you actually
love. Give your mind permission
to blossom during this time.

here now
forgive yourself for
trying to give up
on yourself

you are worth
so much more than you know

Doing the healing work starts with divine knowledge that you are ready to begin the work. Sometimes trauma is too raw to dig into. When we experience something traumatic we go into survival mode—we go numb to the point that sometimes every breath feels like a struggle to take. We need immediate relief. We need to feel safe. We need something to remind us this isn't the end for us. We need someone to reach out to us and we need to reach out to someone for help. We need to know it will be okay. We deserve help. We must remind ourselves we are not a burden. Healing may happen all at once for you or it may happen in different seasons. It may come and pause, then begin again. Only you know what you need. Trust your body. Listen to it. Oftentimes trauma lives within our bodies and shows up before our brain recognizes it's deeply affecting us. We never feel ready to begin the difficult work. It's really, really hard to remember bad memories. But, we are *always* stronger than we give ourselves credit for.

Some people can't help us with our healing because they haven't done the healing work themselves. I hope you don't let someone's inability to help you discourage you from finding the people who can. There are people out there for you. This is your sign to continue searching.

there will be people
who don't see your worth
but that does not mean
you are worthless

As seasons come and go, sometimes people do too, and that is okay. It doesn't mean having them in your life was a mistake. It doesn't mean you messed up too much to be loved the way you know you deserve. It doesn't mean you cannot forgive yourself for allowing them to stay after they hurt you. It doesn't mean you can't forgive them for leaving you if you thought they would stay forever. With every painful season comes a purposeful lesson. Allow the lesson to teach you. Allow the heartbreak to help you love yourself deeper. You have been through so much and your strength runs deep.

I hope you don't let the people who leave you or deeply hurt you define you. I hope you don't let what happens to you define you. Your worth is whole and pure. You are wholesome and wonderful in your own way. The brokenness of someone else doesn't need to leave cracks within you. Let it hurt, let yourself heal, but don't leave yourself empty for too long. You are always more ready to heal than you feel. Fill yourself with love and experiences that remind you why being alive is a blessing. Hold on to the good memories and know that even better memories are coming. And remember: your worth is not within another human, your worth is within you and you alone.

Look inside yourself. Ask yourself what you want and need. Ask yourself why you might be feeling what you're feeling and remind yourself that it's okay if you don't know why. Know that you can move on from anything even if you don't feel ready to. Know that it's okay to not move on right away. Know that it's okay to have no idea what to do. Look inside yourself, you can always find the answers you need. It doesn't have to feel completely right, right away. Sit in the silence of your own presence. Breathe deeply. Start with gratitude if you don't know where to start. Trust that you are being guided.

Not all change feels right, right away. Just because it doesn't feel positive or right doesn't mean it's wrong. Change is uncomfortable and it is overwhelming in so many ways. But without change, you'll never know what's right for you. It is more uncomfortable to be in the same place for too long than it is to step out beyond your fear and just try. Try something new without knowing if it's right. You can always go back, you can always try something different, but at least you can show yourself that you tried.

you don't have to
feel guilty for
needing a long break

Please believe there is still time for you to
be all that you want to be. *There is time.*

...

When you are going through a difficult time, some
people will distance themselves from you, not
because they are bad people, but because they cannot
understand. It's quite possible the people who walk
away from you will regret it later on. *Your worth is
not a reflection of how many people choose to stay.*

...

It's okay to take as many moments as you need for yourself. Take all of the time you need to find your peace of mind.

...

There is someone who will cherish you for the person you are. If you haven't found them yet, let go and let the universe do its work.

...

You are worth loving and you are so worthy of being loved. You deserve someone who will love you with no limits. You are worth loving even on the days you don't feel you've done your best. You are worth loving even when you say something that makes someone upset. An apology is enough for someone who loves you unconditionally—they will understand that maybe it came from a place of pain. They will see you for who you really are and not the words you say. You are worth loving even when you mentally or physically can't love someone the way you want to. You are worthy of being loved by someone who is gentle and patient with you. If you haven't found this person yet, please, don't give up. The growth you can find in lonely seasons is so important.

you are not unlovable
just because one person
doesn't love you like
you wish they would

I don't know what happened to
your heart, but please, don't hold
your love back. There are cracks
that need to be filled with your
love and only your love can fill
them. There are places you need
to go because you deserve the love
you'll find there if you give your
soul permission to explore. You
will know when there is someone
not worth your energy. We are all
worthy of love but only certain souls
are meant to love certain souls. I
don't know what happened to your
heart, but please, keep loving.

Your love is never wasted. Your
love is always seen even if it is not
received to the depth you are giving
it. I don't know what happened
to your heart, but please, remind
yourself that it's okay to need a lot
of time to move on from what hurt
you. It is important to not give your
heart away too soon. It is important
to rest and reflect. It is important
to take time to grow. Growth is
tiring, but growth is so important.

nothing is forever
so please know
things will get better

When you can sense someone you love slowly letting go of their affection for you, I hope you know their lack of love isn't a reflection of your worth. Maybe you hold onto the hope that they will go back to loving you like they did before. Maybe you hold on because you are scared of being lonely yet again. Maybe you hold on because you love this person more than you have ever loved someone before and the reality of them leaving hurts more than you have ever hurt before. People come and go from our lives too easily and too quickly, but this doesn't mean any relationship wasn't worth your energy. The memories you make with people are what makes living life rare and beautiful. The love you gave to someone who left you wasn't worth nothing. The love you gave left imprints on their soul that no matter how easily it seems they get over you, will stay with them eternally. So please, don't ever think your love is wasted. Every bit of love you give impacts someone's soul forever. Thank you for loving people like you do.

You deserve to be loved like
you know you deserve.

...

If you find yourself constantly having to
explain yourself to someone, maybe it's
time to acknowledge they aren't meant to
be in your life. Maybe they aren't meant
to understand you. Maybe someone will
come into your life who will understand
you better than anyone has. You will never
know what is right if you hold on to those
who are wrong. Protect your energy. Let the
wrong people go so the right people can find
you. The people meant to love you will find
you. Letting go will never feel completely
comfortable, but holding on to someone who
isn't right will feel even more uncomfortable.

...

Even if you feel like some people take your love for granted, love is never something to regret giving. Even if loving becomes exhausting, love itself is energy. You know that indescribable feeling you get when you know you helped someone? It's like a certain energy touches your innermost being and you feel warm inside. That is love. Have you experienced those moments when you hit rock bottom but it is only there you experience a presence that reminds you to keep going? That is love. You can always find the willpower to keep loving because love in its purest form has no limits. Love is patience. Love is kindness. Love is compassion and it is healing. It is holding the heart of others without expecting anything in return. Yes, as human beings we need love to survive and we deserve love. I truly believe that the love we give will be returned in whole. Maybe not now. Maybe not in this life, but it is always seen by the One who is guiding us. So please, no matter what—don't stop loving people because you've been hurt. It is okay to feel hurt, neglected, unseen, or anything at all. I promise you, your love is seen. Your love is not worth nothing. *Your love is worth everything.*

you are the reason

someone believes in

the goodness of people

Thank you for loving people the way you do. Even if you don't feel it, you are so appreciated and your love is never wasted.

...

You deserve someone who will show up for you the way you show up for them. I hope you seek patience in the process of finding love. I hope you hold your standards high because you do deserve what you desire.

...

It's okay. It's okay. It will be okay.

...

Rest. Be extra gentle with your heart and
mind. Do something that brings you joy.
Do what you can and know that is enough.
Slow down. Exercise if you can, but don't be
too hard on yourself if that's too much. Get
outside, but don't be too hard on yourself
if that's too much. Drink water. Soak in the
shower. Eat what you want to eat. Fill your
body with nutrients too. Let go of guilt. Let
go of the pressure you put on yourself to
be okay all of the time. Give yourself love.
Nurture yourself. There is nothing wrong with
you. You deserve to do anything you need to
do to feel at peace. Take care of yourself.

...

as it has passed before

it will this time

too

What you are going through is temporary.
Keep holding on. Your life is so important.

...

Sometimes all you can do is breathe
and tell yourself to let it go and those
two seconds change everything.

...

You are completely enough,
just as you are.

...

It will get better even if it
doesn't seem like it will.

...

When you're feeling like a burden to the
people around you, remember the moments
you brought them joy. Remember the
moments you made someone laugh or the
moments you helped someone out. Remember
the moments you felt like you belonged—not
the moments you feel like you don't belong
anywhere. You do belong everywhere you
are. Remember, humans need humans and
humans want to be there for their people.
I hope you learn to like the human being
that you are. I hope you learn to speak to
yourself gently. I hope you learn to give
yourself credit. I hope you remind yourself
of your worth when you're feeling unworthy
of being where you are. You are beyond
worthy of taking up space. People love you
where you are and want you around. You
have never been too much of anything.

...

Do not give your energy away to anyone who
doesn't treat you like you're enough.

...

Don't you see that the peace you've been
looking for has been within you all along?

...

Sometimes, the bravest thing you can do
is forgive your heart for hurting.

...

You can.

You can do what you think you can't. You can
prove them wrong. You can prove yourself
wrong. You can move on from the people
and memories you think you can't move
on from. You can find a kind of love that
makes you understand what it means to
hold someone who takes your breath away.
Someone who makes you laugh until you can
hardly breathe. Someone who is so tender
that you find yourself holding your breath
wondering how they ever became yours. You
can accomplish what you think you can't.

You can live your life not depending on
others. You can live your life without allowing
the opinions of others to dictate what you
do with your life. You can go about your
day not worrying about being consumed by
what others think. It's your life, not theirs.
It's your decision, not theirs. You can grow
to be the person you know you are meant
to be despite what any other voice says.

I'm so proud of you for doing
your best to be okay.
I'm so proud of you for waking up everyday
and trying. I'm so proud of you for being here
today because I know some of your yesterdays
were really hard. I don't know what you're
going through but you are going to get through
it. You are going to get through whatever you're
going through. I hope you fight for yourself
when no one else does and I hope you know
you are worthy of your wildest dreams. You
are someone worth fighting for. Keep going.

...

Thank you for being the person who
makes people feel okay when they're
not okay. The world truly is a kinder
place because you are in it.

...

sending love to anyone
who has lost
a loved one

*this is your sign that
the one you lost
is still with you*

You will find whole healing.

...

Even the moments that seem insignificant now may mean something for later. You are growing within your relationships and most importantly—you are growing within yourself. You are always being prepared. You are always more capable than you think. You are learning to trust yourself and the silent voice of your soul that is your instincts, your protection. You are learning how to receive what you need and that is so powerful. Lessons you are learning now, you will carry with you forever. It is in seasons of struggle we get to know ourselves the best. Getting through isn't about just getting through. Getting through is an opportunity for personal growth. So when you are in a season of struggle, ask yourself this, *"How am I growing through this and what is my struggle trying to teach me?"*

...

Your hard work will pay off. Maybe not
soon, but someday you will see that your
efforts meant something all along.

...

Be productive at your own
pace—not the world's pace.

...

You are allowed to genuinely enjoy your
life. You should never feel guilty for being
happy. Taking care of yourself sometimes
means not always being the one to worry
about others. Because if you're always
worrying about others, you will never
find the happiness that you deserve.

...

some reminders for you

Tell the people you love that you love them.
Tell the people who have been there for you
that you couldn't have gotten through without
them. Remind them they are appreciated.
Ask the people you care about if they are
okay if you think they might not be. Check
in with the people who are always checking
in with others. Be kind to those who aren't
kind. Forgive those who won't forgive you.
Let go of those who you know are toxic and
trust that you will find the best kind of people
for you. Be there for others but be there for
yourself first. Be yourself, not anyone else.

Watching someone you love lose someone they love is hard. Their pain becomes your pain. Their grief, in a way, becomes your grief. Watching their heart ache and their eyes dry of tears is difficult to experience. It's this awkward yet powerful experience of learning to love them in a way that is completely selfless. It's almost like an out-of-body experience. You have to let go of your needs for some time and wrap yourself in their needs. You have to take care of them knowing that in this situation, taking care of them is taking care of yourself. You learn so much about your capacity for compassion. You learn so much about your love for them. You learn the power of rest. You learn the strength every soul has within to be carried through grief.

If you are loving someone through their grief, remember that having nothing to say is okay. Remember to trust that your spirit will guide you when you are speechless. Remember that just being there for them and holding them when they need to be held is powerful. Remember that it is okay to feel deep sadness, too. It's okay to cry with them. It's okay to need other people's support. It's okay to need to be held through it too. Giving all of your compassion and care to someone is draining. Be there for yourself, too. You get through it the best you can together and in the end, it brings you closer together.

you don't have
to have it all together
all of the time

When was the last time you said to someone,
I am so grateful you are in my life.

...

I hope you embrace the moments you feel good.
I hope you know the moments you don't feel
good will lead to inner transformation. I hope
you know you deserve to be genuinely happy
and excited about your life. You deserve to be
proud of the happiness you've found. I hope
you find wonder in learning something new
everyday. I hope you remember to check in with
the people you care about. I hope you mindfully
save your money to take the trip you've always
wanted to take. I hope you know money doesn't
define you. I hope you remember the old saying
that money doesn't buy happiness. I hope you
work hard but take breaks often. I hope you
put yourself first. Yes, life really is too short

....

It's okay to feel confused. It's okay to feel
overwhelmed. It's okay to worry about what
others are thinking. It's okay to take your time.
It's okay to step away from the beliefs you've
been told to believe. It's okay to be figuring
out what you believe. Through the process
you are discovering the truth of who you are.
Allow the process to flow as it is flowing. Open
up when you are ready to open up. Surrender
to who you are. Trust in who you are.

...

Life isn't about how much you get done
every day. Life is meant to be lived in a way
that fills you with a collection of moments
that make you so grateful to exist.

...

Chaos in the world doesn't have to create chaos in your heart. Give your heart permission to let peace in. Sit in the silence with your breath and remind yourself that you are safe. You are separate from the world around you. You are in control of how you react to anything outside of yourself. Within you, you hold peace. Within you, you hold divine knowledge. In this moment, connect with yourself. Place your hand on your heart and thank it for bringing you to this moment. There will always be chaos in the world, but the more we practice recognizing our inner peace, the more we will be able to find peace in the world and the more we will be able to spread peace into the world.

...

You were handed the life you are living because you are strong enough to live it.

...

Not everything happens for a reason, but
everything that happens offers an opportunity
for reflection and growth. How did you
change for the better? How can your change
help change someone else for the better?

...

You are on a journey and every experience is
leading you to where you belong. It's really hard
to see and trust when you're living through
the awkwardness of the unknown, but you are
exactly where you're meant to be right now.
You are experiencing everything you are meant
to be. Not everything happens for a reason but
everything that happens can lead to a deep
lesson and change. Doors that are meant for you
will open for you. Doors don't open until our
souls live through and grow through what we
go through. One day you will come to a door
when you least expect it and it will open. You
will be filled with a new light. Until then, be
where you are now. Ask your soul to show you
what you need to know. "I open my heart to the
lessons intended for me. I am deeply growing."

...

For the one feeling lonely...

Maybe this is your time to get to know yourself better and to learn to be patient with the parts of yourself you wish were not a part of you. Maybe you are supposed to feel this loneliness so that you can start to rely on yourself more than others. You are the most powerful influence in your life—you must start taking care of yourself accordingly. I hope you know it is never selfish to put yourself first. No matter how uncomfortable being alone can be, I hope you start to see that the moments of your loneliness are the moments you grew the most. How are you getting to know yourself better?

The timing of your life is perfect.
One day your door will open.

...

This is your reminder to not let your
loneliness make you choose toxic people.

...

If you need to rest, rest.
If you need to cry, cry.
If you need to move, move.
If you don't know what you need, that is okay too.

...

Give yourself all of the time you need today to just be there for yourself. Don't pay attention to the people who judge you for needing to do what's best for you. You don't need anyone's approval when it comes to taking care of yourself. More than anything though, don't judge yourself. You are allowed to feel what you're feeling. You will figure out what you need, but you don't need to know what that is at this very moment. Let your feelings flow.

...

It will all work out. You will become who you need to be. You will find what you are looking for.

...

You're not supposed to be the best you can
be all the time. This time of not feeling like
yourself will pass, remind yourself of that.
Feeling out of it could be your mind telling
you it's time for a break, no matter how
long it takes. You will find your way back
to yourself. Until then, don't be hard on
yourself. You're doing the best you can.

...

It is not too late to do the things you
wish you had done by now.

...

You do not owe anyone an explanation
for being how you are.

...

There will be people who come into your life that disturb it. Sometimes, in the most miraculous way. Other times, in the most devastating way. Maybe someone has come into your life who helped tear down your walls just to leave you alone to build them up again. Maybe someone has come into your life who changed you in the best way and the worst way all at once. Maybe someone came in and left, leaving you losing faith in relationships and people all together. Maybe you are worn out and so close to giving up on relationships even though you don't want to. Maybe you aren't ready to let go of someone even though you know it is time to. I hope you don't lose yourself trying to hold onto someone else. I hope you give your heartache permission to teach you. You will never be the same in relationships again and maybe that's not a bad thing. Maybe you will learn what it means to be treated in the way you've always been told you deserve. Maybe you will appreciate the people who come into your life for the first time even more than you would have before. Maybe you will see that, even though not everything happens for a reason, through everything can come something beautiful. Light always comes after dark.

if something doesn't feel right
don't do it

The people who judge you are not secure within
themselves. If they were, they would know
kindness is the only way to treat someone.

...

You will find your soulmate when you are
meant to, there is nothing wrong with you.

...

Even though there are people who don't stay in your
life forever, maybe they made your life beautiful in
some way, and that is important to remember.

...

There are people who will come into your life that shift your future. Some for better, some for worse. But don't dwell too long on those who made your life worse. Remember the ones who cared that didn't need to. Remember the ones who carried you when you couldn't get up. The ones who loved you without knowing you. The ones who helped you when you didn't know you needed them. The ones who showed kindness when you needed it most. There are people you don't even remember today that are a reason you are where you are. There are people out there who remember you because of the impact you made on them. Your life is special and your life is important. Even when you feel alone, you won't be left alone. Even when you can't hold yourself together, someone will be there to keep you safe.

it's quite possible
them leaving you
or you leaving them
saved your life

Meet yourself where you're at right now. Your past isn't who you are or where you are. Your future isn't who you are or where you are. You are not defined by what you accomplish. You are defined by how you treat yourself and others. You are full of goodness. Goodness is here right now. Wholeness is here right now. You are here right now... Meet yourself. You are worthy of accepting yourself for who you are right now. You are worthy of giving yourself space and grace. So when you overthink, meet yourself. When you're doubting, meet yourself. When you're insecure, meet yourself. When you're trying to rush the future, meet yourself. When your thoughts are living in the past, meet yourself here, now. Be here, now. Feel what you feel, here now. Feel the stillness in the air around you. Breathe in grace, breathe out tension. You are here. *You belong where you are.*

Meet yourself where you're at.

...

You will find what you are looking for and you will
become who you need to be. It will all work out.

...

You will find your way to where you belong.

...

You are not any less than the people you think are better than you. You are not too far behind your peers. You haven't missed out on too much. You aren't taking too much time to get to where you belong. You will not always feel lost. You will not always feel like you're the only one falling behind. You will not always question if you even belong anywhere. Give your heart permission to guide you. Trust in the One guiding you. Your spirit is wise. Breathe through the negative chatter in your mind. Instead of asking, "What am I doing with my life?" ask, "What is one thing I can do today that is purposeful?" That one thing could be reading an article about a topic you're interested in learning about. It could be showing kindness to a stranger. It could be cooking a delicious meal for someone you love. It could be sharing words online in hope to make someone feel less alone or encouraged. If we don't feel a sense of purpose, we can't move forward. Every single human being has a purpose. We all have something we're naturally good at. Follow that. Even if it doesn't become a sustainable job, that's okay. Just please don't lose sight of what makes you feel the most alive. What makes you feel most alive is part of your purpose in this life.

I hope you know that you are doing
better than you think you are.

...

We are all going through something
simultaneously. We are all connected.
We are all doing the best we can. Let's
keep doing the best we can—that is
enough. *Every single second where you
are, as you are, is more than enough.*

...

Your hard work will pay off. Your efforts are
not wasted and you have so much to be proud
of. Don't you see how far you have come?

...

I hope you choose to fight for yourself instead of against yourself. I hope you choose to not hold on to the hurt, but instead work on the hurt so that you can live the life you dream about. I am not saying forgive and forget. Pain often leaves permanent wounds, but those wounds will never turn into scars if you never forgive, and the thing about scars is... Scars don't hurt. Too many people walk around ignoring their wounds and live a life in a constant fight with themselves. Life is not supposed to be a repetitive struggle. Life is supposed to be an enjoyable and beautiful experience that fills your soul with more sunshine than rain. You deserve to fight for yourself and you deserve people who will fight for you. You are worth someone's complete attention and care, but this is your reminder that you are also worth your own. Give yourself all the time and attention you need to heal. You are doing better than you think you are.

you will get to where
you need to be

We are all going through something simultaneously. We are all connected. We are all doing the best we can. Let's keep doing the best we can—that is enough. *Every single second where you are, as you are, is more than enough.*

...

It's time to focus on yourself and no one else. Stop taking care of everyone else before you take care of yourself. Stop just trying to just get by in this life. What do you want? What do you need? What is best for you? Choosing yourself is never selfish. Before you can be the best you can be for anyone else you have to be the best you can be for yourself.

...

It's not too late to do the things you
wish you would have done by now.

...

Keep pushing through for yourself. You deserve
to make it through. Keep pushing through
for the possibility that you will end up happy.
Keep pushing through for the possibility that
you will make your way to where you belong.
Keep pushing through for the good moments
you will have with people you know care about
you. Keep pushing through to see your healing
through. You will come through to the other
side of it and be in awe of yourself. Not in
a selfish way, but in a strong way. You hold
so much strength within you. Keep pushing
through for the possibility you will see why
you went through what you're going through.
You have been through too much to not see
yourself through it—you are someone who
has the heart to change a part of the world.

...

Tell the people you love that you love them.
Call the people back you've been ignoring.
Slow down. Do the things you want to do
if you can do them. Say hello to the people
you're nervous to talk to. Hug the people
in your life like you may never hug them
again. Love harder. Let go of being hard on
yourself. Remember the good memories
when bad memories are holding your heart
too tight. Remember how far you have
come. Take care of yourself the most so you
can take care of the people you care about
more. Be really kind and be really loving.
Remember that you are so loved and peace
will always hold you when you need it.

I hope you learn to love the person you have become. In the moments when you are alone I hope you learn that you have everything within you to comfort yourself. You don't always have to lean on another human for comfort. You don't have to search for outside sources to find peace. It's uncomfortable to be alone when you're not used to it. It's uncomfortable to sit in the silence with your own presence and just be. But, one of the best, most life-changing things you can learn is to be alone. To love your own presence. To not need another human to make you feel better. Once you learn to love and take care of yourself, you can do anything. You can change your life. You can live your life in a way that doesn't fill your soul with regrets. You can go to bed every evening and be proud of something that you did that day, even if it feels small.

There is something to be proud of every day even if it's *just* making it through the day— that is something to always be proud of.

This is your sign that
you can,
you must,
you should keep going.

...

I hope you fall in love with yourself before
you give anyone else your love. I hope you
see yourself as someone worth adoring.
Nothing about you is a mistake. Nothing
about you is even close to worthless.
Your worth is not conditional.
You are someone no one else is and that
is your power. You are someone everyone
should treat with nothing but goodness—if
they don't, they are not worthy of you.

...

You will find yourself looking back on your pain and recognize the strength you found that pulled you through. You will be filled with peace in every part of your being. You will smile to yourself in awe knowing you made it through what seemed impossible to get through too many times. Every second you are healing. Every breath you take sends energy to your body that wants to heal you. Healing is a wave. It comes and goes. It shouldn't happen too soon. It should take time, even though time is uncomfortable. We want it to happen overnight. We want to forget and move on. Give your healing permission to come and go. You will have breakthroughs and then periods of stillness. Your emotions will hit hard or won't hit at all. It isn't supposed to make sense. Through it all we must take a step back and watch ourselves be the wave knowing we will end up okay.

I hope you know the world is
better because you are in it.

...

It's okay to be struggling even if it seems
others are struggling more. It's okay to put
yourself first even if you tell yourself it's
selfish. It's okay to not always be the strong
one. It's okay to not know what to say in
every situation. It's okay to be exhausted and
need time alone. It's okay to rest. It's okay to
need other people. Your experience is worthy
of attention and nurturing. Your experience
is valid. You are not selfish for feeling what
you're feeling. Don't compare your experience
to theirs. You're experiencing a lot too.

...

Even if you don't feel content where you are, I am so proud of you for being where you are. You have overcome more than so many people know. Maybe there was a time you didn't think you would make it, but here you are. You made it and you will continue to make it. You deserve to live the life you want to live, not the life others expect you to live. You deserve to be proud of the person you are and love the life you are living.

You are not a failure for not being
where you think you should be.

...

I hope you don't lose yourself trying to
prove yourself to everyone else. You have
nothing to prove to anyone, really. Really,
if at the end of the day you can say you
tried your best that day, that is more than
enough. Your best won't look the same
everyday and that is more than okay. People
can think all that they want about you, but
the opinions of others don't define you.

...

Figuring your life out won't happen
overnight, because it shouldn't. Part of
the process is finding patience with the
process. You will start to know what to
do or where to go once you truly let go.

...

You are going to figure it out but you don't
have to figure it out right now.

...

You can do what you think you
can't. You can prove them wrong.
You can prove yourself wrong. You
can move on from the people and
memories you think you can't move
on from. You can find a kind of
love that makes you understand
what it means to hold someone who
takes your breath away. Someone
who makes you laugh until you
can hardly breathe. Someone who
is so tender that you find yourself
holding your breath wondering how
they ever became yours. You can
accomplish what you think you can't.

You have been through so much and you got
through it—you will get through this, too.
It will all be okay. What doesn't make sense
now will make sense someday. You will end
up where you belong. You will end up with
who you belong with. You will find what
you're looking for when you are meant to find
it. Everything doesn't happen for a reason,
but you can find a reason to keep going no
matter what happens. You are learning. You
are growing. You are not your mistakes.
You are not what other people think of
you. You are what you think of yourself.

Stop comparing your life to everyone
else's. You are only holding yourself back
trying to be someone other than yourself.
Speak to yourself the way you think about
the people you're comparing yourself to.
You are just as talented. You are just as
inspiring. You are just as worthy of the
life you dream of because you are the only
you that exists—this is your power.

...

No matter what you are feeling
today, the good or the bad, you are
seen and loved and never alone.

...

You won't find the happiness you are looking for by being so hard on yourself. Negative thoughts only lead to negative places. Positive thoughts lead to action and action leads to change. Even if you don't know if what you want to happen can happen, breathe life into it. Use the power of your mind and your thinking to bring it to life. The Universe responds positively to positive energy.

be really gentle
with yourself

I hope you know you don't have to
apologize for anything that means
you are putting yourself first.

...

Please, be strong in who you are. And please,
don't let the actions of another convince you
that you are not good enough as you are.

...

You are worth so much more than what people say about you. If someone has ever spoken badly about your work, your relationships, your beliefs, etc.—trust what you know. Trust who you are. Trust that you are doing what's best for you and the people who believe in you, whether they understand your choices or not, are the people for you. It is okay if those people are not your family members. It is okay if those people are only your family members. It is okay to create your own version of a family if your family doesn't treat you the way you deserve to be. It is okay if right now you are the only person who believes in the path meant for you. It is okay to try new things. It is okay to choose yourself over anyone else. *You should always choose yourself.*

it is completely okay to
take as many moments as
you need for yourself

I hope you learn to be alone and
love every version of yourself. I hope
you learn to let go of what has hurt
you and believe that good times
are coming. Time is only running
out if you aren't living your life
the way you want to. Life is more
precious than we realize—don't
take advantage of the gift that
everyday is. You deserve to be the
happiest version of yourself, the
most content version of yourself,
the most alive version of yourself.

Good, genuine, incredible people
will come into your life sooner than
it feels like. They will help you heal
in ways you didn't know you needed
and they won't even realize the
impact they're making. It will be a
precious connection. Until then, this
is the time to learn to be content
with being alone. This is the time to
learn that you don't need anyone to
be everything you need. This is the
time to learn that you always have
everything you need within you.

If you don't want to regret your life, you cannot live it trying to please others. You cannot live it trying to prove to the world that you meet its (unrealistic) success status. Success shouldn't be about how much you get done in a day. Success shouldn't be about how many people like you or follow you. Success should always and only be about the positive impact you make. How are you making the world a better place? No matter if you love your job or don't like it at all, you can still be kind to the people you interact with. You can still put a smile on someone's face. You can still be the positive energy the environment around you needs.

Finding your way through your
healing can bring to life growth
like nothing else can. The kind of
growth that, through how strong
you become, helps others through
their healing. The kind of growth
that inspires you to live every breath
you take with gratitude. You will be
shown what it means to live your
life never taking it for granted. You
will be shown what it means to fall
in with yourself before anyone else.
You will be shown so many things
you never knew were possible. You
will be someone that no one can
break and you will be someone you
finally believe is worth nothing
but goodness. *You are worthy of
everything you don't think you deserve.*

Do the thing you've been wanting to do. Let go of the fear that it might be too hard or it might be the wrong thing to do. You can always go back to where you were if it doesn't work out. Starting over doesn't need to be as intimidating as we tell ourselves it will be. New beginnings are more than just a fresh start. New beginnings are an offering to finally find the peace you've been needing. The choices and decisions you make are a reflection of your journey thus far. You know what you know and with that, you do the best you can to decipher right from wrong. Every breath you take is a second chance. It's not too late for you.

I am sending a prayer of love to those
who aren't feeling like themselves right
now. I am sending a prayer of comfort
to those who feel lonely. I am sending
a prayer of energy to those who don't
have energy. I am sending a prayer of
protection to those who don't feel safe
where they are. I am sending a prayer
of peace to those who have anxiety.
I am sending a prayer of joy to those
who are experiencing depression. I
am sending a prayer of overwhelming
gratitude to those who are kind. I am
sending a prayer of love to those who
don't feel loved. I am sending a prayer
of grace to those who feel resentful,
angry, unforgiving, or judgmental.
I am saying a prayer that all souls
experience love, comfort, protection,
energy, joy, peace, and gratitude.

JACQUELINE WHITNEY
is a writer from Philadelphia, Pennsylvania. Her
words are a daily source of comfort for many.

THOUGHT CATALOG Books

Thought Catalog Books is a publishing imprint of Thought Catalog, a digital magazine for thoughtful storytelling, and is owned and operated by The Thought & Expression Company, an independent media group based in Brooklyn, NY. Founded in 2010, we are committed to helping people become better communicators and listeners to engender a more exciting, attentive, and imaginative world. As a publisher and media platform, we help creatives all over the world realize their artistic vision and share it in print and digital forms with audiences across the globe.

ThoughtCatalog.com | **Thoughtful Storytelling**

ShopCatalog.com | **Shop Books + Curated Products**

**MORE FROM
THOUGHT CATALOG BOOKS**

Beyond Worthy
—Jacqueline Whitney

The Mountain Is You
—Brianna Wiest

Everything You'll Ever Need
(You Can Find Within Yourself)
—Charlotte Freeman

A Gentle Reminder
—Bianca Sparacino

THOUGHT
CATALOG
Books

THOUGHTCATALOG.COM
NEW YORK · LOS ANGELES